HE MADE IT ALL
A Rhyming Creation Story

As told by
LaBena Fleming

Part of
"God Said" Series

Copyright © [2025] [LaBena Fleming]
All rights reserved.

No part of this publication may be reproduced, shared, or transmitted in any form or by any means, including photocopying, recording, or other electronic/mechanical methods, without LaBena Fleming's explicit written express permission.

Illustrations by Joseph Martins

Editing by Becci Murray

DEDICATION

This work was inspired by God and is dedicated to all of His children.

With love to my granddaughter Tia Z, and with thanks to a special young reader, Harley C.

He Made

It All

DAY ONE

In the beginning was nothing but God,
He created the heavens and Earth.
The earth was quite formless and empty
And so he decided to build up its worth.

The spirit of God drifted over dark waters,
And there he said, "Let there be light."
Dividing the darkness from all that sprang forth,
He called the light Day and dark Night.
Genesis 1:1-5

DAY TWO

As God separated the vast earthly waters
From heavenly ones, far and wide,
He also created a space between them,
Then God smiled, and he called it the sky.
Genesis 1:6-8

God said,
"Let all of the land produce seed-bearing plants,
And trees that will grow lots of fruit."
He planted them all in their various kinds,
Where they started to grow and take root.

The land produced all kinds of different plants,
Even those that we now use as food,
And God looked at everything he had created,
And saw his creation was good.
Genesis 1:9-13

DAY FOUR

God said,
"Let there be lights in the space of the sky,
That will separate daytime from night,
And let them both shine and so mark sacred times,
Days and years that will make the earth bright."

So then two great lights were created by God,
One each for the day and the night.
The big one called Sun, and the little one Moon.
Both were precious in God's holy sight.

Then God made the stars in the space he called Sky,
To help separate day from the dark.
The lights then took charge of the night and the day,
Now displaying God's own special mark.
Genesis 1:14-18

DAY FIVE

God said,
"Let great moving creatures all fill up the waters,
And let birds begin now to fly,"
So, of their own kind, he created them all,
And they filled up the seas and the sky.

He created great whales and all other sea creatures
That moved through the earth's open waters.
He made octopuses, the squid, and the fish,
And then later, their sons and their daughters.

And all living things that filled up the vast seas
Moved according to their own kind.
God saw they were good, and he blessed each with love,
Every creature you ever could find.

DAY SIX

God said,
"Let land now produce lots of new living creatures,
According to their own kind.
The cattle and beasts, and the small creeping things,"
And whatever else came to his mind.

"Now let us make man in our very own image,
And let them rule each living thing,
The lions, the lambs, all the fish and the frogs,
Even small buzzing bees that can sting."

And so God made man in his very own image,
Both male and female, he made them,
And gave them control over all that he'd made
As they ruled on his earthly kingdom.

"Be fruitful and multiply," God told them both,
As he gave man his love and his blessing.
"Replenish the earth and the sky and the seas,"
For his faithful love he was expressing.

God said,
"Now, do you see all these things I have made?
You may have them to use as your food,"
And when God looked over at all he'd created,
He saw that it was very good.
Genesis 1:24-31

DAY SEVEN

The heavens and Earth were created by God,
Yes, in all of their great vast array.
This marvelous work God was able to do
Before reaching the seventh day.

He looked all around at his fine handiwork,
Knowing this was his absolute best,
And blessing the seventh day, God smiled and said,
"Let today be my one day of rest."
Genesis 2:2-3

So now you have learned this incredible story
Of how God created the earth,
And all living things that are on and above it,
Their value, their grace, and their worth.

We must treat our dear world with kindness and love,
We must handle this planet with care.
With love and with goodness, the earth was created,
For all of God's people to share.

Yes, God has entrusted the whole earth to us,
And all creatures, the great and the small,
So always take care of the world around you,
And remember that He made it all.

ACTIVITY

1. Have the children draw a picture of their favorite thing in nature.
2. Have the children explain why it's their favorite thing.
3. Have children discuss how to protect their favorite thing.

www.ingramcontent.com/pod-product-compliance
Lightning Source LLC
Chambersburg PA
CBHW041525070526
44585CB00002B/85